Greater Than a Tourist – Bologna, Emilia-Romagna Region, Italy

50 Travel Tips from a Local

> TOURIST

Emily Mathews

Lock Haven, PA

ISBN: 9781521265475

DEDICATION

This book is dedicated to A.T., the greatest thing that's ever come from Bologna; even better than tortellini!

BOOK DESCRIPTION

Are you excited about planning your next trip?
Do you want to try something new while traveling?
Would you like some guidance from a local?

If you answered yes to any of these questions, then this book is just for you.

Greater Than a Tourist – Bologna, Italy by Emily Mathews offers the inside scoop on Bologna.
Most travel books tell you how to travel like a tourist. Although there's nothing wrong with that, as a part of the Greater than a Tourist series this book will give you tips and a bunch of ideas from someone who lives at your next travel destination.

In these pages you'll discover local advice that will help you throughout your stay. Greater than a Tourist is a series of travel books written by locals.
Travel like a local. Get the inside scoop. Slow down, stay in one place, take your time, get to know the people and the culture of a place. Try some things off the beaten path with guidance. Patronize local business and vendors when you travel. Be willing to try something new and have the travel experience of a lifetime.

By the time you finish this book, you will be excited to travel to your next destination.

So grab YOUR copy today. You'll be glad you did.

CONTENTS

> TOURIST

Author Bio

Emily Mathews graduated from Vassar College in 1993 and planned to go adventuring in Europe the next day. Things didn't go quite the way she expected, and it wasn't until 2001 that she was able to head to Bologna, Italy "just for a few months." Then THAT didn't go quite the way she expected, and she wound up living there for over 14 years!

Emily loves spending time with her daughter, speaking Italian (so it doesn't get rusty) writing, and she is developing a penchant for DIY art projects. She also acts as staff member to an inscrutable black cat named Mildred who hails from a feral colony in the hills around Bologna.

And of course, she's wondering what next great adventure isn't going to go quite the way she expects!

...

WELCOME TO > TOURIST

EMILY MATHEWS

WHY AM I A LOCAL?

Having lived in Bologna for over 14 years, I can tell you that this is a city where you can taste the very best cuisine Italy has to offer. Italians from everywhere on the peninsula agree that the food in Bologna is truly spectacular.

In every way, how and what you eat will characterize your time here, from where you do your marketing in the morning and your choice of wine in the afternoon, to when you meet and how you organize your weekend plans.

I love Bologna because the natives are proud, and reserved, and open to newcomers, all at the same time. They themselves will tour their own city, so pleased with themselves to have discovered something they hadn't known about it before.

In Bologna, you have the luxury of enjoying one of the European Capital of Culture cities (2000) while simultaneously experiencing the intimacy of its cozy, small-town atmosphere.

Bologna is well known for its university, its politics, its architecture, its music, and infinitely more. But I also enjoy its weekly market, its relative quiet in August, and the sense that the cobbles and archways themselves seem to have a story to tell.

I moved to Bologna, Italy when I was 30 years old. Bologna is where I learned Italian. Nothing pleases me more than when Italians look at me after we've started talking and say, "Wait. You're not Italian! But you learned our language in Bologna!"

Come with me and see what I learned in Bologna, while I was becoming a local...

EMILY MATHEWS

1. *Find a Place to Stay (and Learn Some Italian Too!)*

Worried about finding a decent place to rest your head and wondering how you're going to explain this in Italian? Never fear! Check out Cultura Italiana, Italian Language School, right in the heart of Bologna. The course offerings are vast and taught by native speakers, and they will help you find accommodations for the duration of the time you are a student with them. It's a great way to get to know about real life in Bologna, and you'll be chatting and living like a local in no time!

2. *Buy Groceries, Just Like a Local*

So you have a place to stay, but you don't want to eat out for every meal. You need to go to the supermarket!. The center of Bologna has quite a few supermarkets and mini-markets, but if you have the time, the best quality and prices are at Esselunga. There is one on the Via Emilia Ponente: Esselunga Santa Viola. It's not right downtown, but it won't take you more than a 15-minute bus ride to get there, and besides, it's where the locals do their marketing for everyday things. The number 13 local and the 81, 87, and 91 express busses (just to name a few) stop there for the standard bus fare from the center. You can watch the locals and see what they put in their shopping carts to feed their families. Just remember that you will need a 1 EURO coin to put into your own shopping cart in order to use it, but you'll get your money back when you put the buggy back with the rest of them. Oh, and last but not least, Italian supermarkets like Esselunga aren't usually open all day Sunday (unless it's during the holidays) so get your shopping done between 9 a.m. and 2 p.m. The rest of the week, it's business as usual.

3. *Get Your Food from an Old Fashioned Italian Market*

Perhaps you're more in the mood for a farmers' market atmosphere, picking up only what you'll be needing for that day's meals. In that case, stop in at Mercato delle Erbe, Via Ugo Bassi, 25. Open Monday through Saturday, each vendor is a shopping experience unto itself. You'll have your choice of fruit and vegetable sellers, multiple options for meats and cheeses, and if you happen to get hungry while you're there, you can stop in one of the eateries that line the inside perimeter of the market. You'll see Italians of all ages there, from ancient grandmothers shopping for beloved grandchildren, to modern business women stopping in for two artichokes and some fresh bread to make a light meal that evening. And lucky you! You'll walk away with the freshest ingredients for whatever you've got cooking!

4. *Make Sure You Have the Right Wine*

No trip to anywhere in Italy would be complete without wine, but it can be a little daunting. The choices are endless, as is the range of prices. But as with all things wine, the Italians have a solution! You can go to the supermarket and wander their wine aisle, confident that you will get a good product. Each wine is described in detail on the price tag, which will also tell you what the wine should be served with. If the prospect of having to decipher the language before committing to the purchase is overwhelming, most Italians are usually quite happy to assist. You need only indicate if the wine is for "pranzo" (lunch) or "cena" (supper) and how much you want to spend. But you don't have to break the bank. I've gotten really good wines to serve or to bring as hostess gifts for about 4 EURO which were absolutely lovely.

5. Make an Event Out of Choosing Your Liquors

If you want an education on wine and spirits, you could go to one of the myriad enoteche in Bologna. These shops sell both high and modestly priced wines, and many also offer a variety of grappas and non-Italian spirits as well. The fun comes from being in the presence of experts who will school the shopper in the flavors and perfumes of the drink in question, and often times there will be light snacks offered too. It's an outing in and of itself, and a pleasant way to pass an afternoon.

6. Eat Pizza at a Pizzeria

So what would a trip to Italy be without pizza? Hardly a trip at all. Keep in mind that you rarely order pizza by the slice in Italy. When you eat pizza, you get the whole pie to yourself. It sounds a little intimidating at first, but somehow folks always manage to eat the whole thing! You've got plenty of options in Bologna, but the best by far is Bella Napoli, on Via San Felice. Don't let the less-than-warm wait staff or the relatively small pizza put you off. That's just the way the pizza is at Bella Napoli, and every bite is delicious. And a word to the wise for those of you who are just learning the language, "peperoni" means peppers. If you want a pepperoni pizza, you need to order "salame piccante." I learned that the hard (funny) way! Oh, and don't forget that you DON'T tip! Waiting table is a respected profession, and your bill will include a "coperta" for every person in your party.

7. Order Take-Out

If you prefer take-out, pizza is king, but most take-aways have whole meals on the menu as well. Delivery is almost always included within a certain radius of the storefront, and more often than not, if you order over a certain EURO amount, or more than a certain number of pizzas they'll throw in a bottle of soda. You can usually order beer as well. Now as for where to place your order, that will depend on where you are in the city, but I have to recommend Fatt' na Pizz on Via Emilia Ponente. (It's a little farther on, past the Esselunga Santa Viola.) The ingredients are always fresh, the combinations they've put together are delicious, the portions are huge (easily providing another meal in leftovers) and the staff are friendly and helpful. Again, tipping is rare in Italy, and this includes the delivery person. But if the weather is particularly bad, a EURO per pizza or meal (and a bottle of water in the Summertime) is always appreciated.

8. Give the Gift of Chocolate

Food is always much appreciated in Italy, anytime, anywhere. So if you have the great good fortune to be invited to someone's home for a meal but don't know what to bring, a box of Majani chocolates goes over quite nicely. This is one of Bologna's culinary treasures, recognized the world over for its quality. While the factory has since moved into the countryside on the outskirts of Bologna, the shop is right in the center at Via De' Carbonesi, 5. Walking in is like going back in time, with individual boxes wrapped and festooned with ribbons. And you won't be surrounded by tourists either. This is where the Bolognesi go to find special confections for special occasions, from Christmas goodies to Easter eggs. Keep in mind that this shop, and many others in Bologna, shut down for an extended lunch hour Monday – Wednesday, Friday, and Saturday, as well as the whole of Thursday afternoons, and Sundays.

9. Enjoy More Sweets at the Cioccoshow

Every November, right around the middle of the month, Bologna hosts a chocolate festival known as the Cioccoshow. Chocolate vendors from all over the world descend on Piazza Maggiore, transforming the entire area into a white-tented labyrinth, and a little corner of heaven on earth. There are chocolate covered, candied fruits and nuts, and chains of chocolate salami. There are chocolate sculptures, and chocolate fountains, and it feels like you're walking in a chocolate scented cloud. It's easy to get lost among the stalls, but that might not be so bad!

10. Do a Gelato Taste Test

If you go to Bologna in the warmer months, you may need that queen of all ice-creams, gelato. The Bolognesi claim to have the best of the best in their fair city, and they may be right, but why not taste for yourself! The choices abound. You can try Gelateria Ugo on Via San Felice, and don't let the shop's tiny dimensions fool you: big flavors await within! There is Gelateria Gianni on Via Monetegrappa where the names of the flavors are as creative and varied as the gelato itself. And there's my personal favorite, La Sorbetteria Castiglione on Via Castiglione. But whichever you choose, you will find locals in every single one, because these are the places where the Bolognesi go for their gelato.

EMILY MATHEWS

"Bologna is famous for producing popes, painters, and sausage." – Lord Byron

11. Eat Like You're in a Local's Own Kitchen

Looking for a place to have a traditional meal out? There is no lack of options in Bologna, but I highly recommend the Bolognese cuisine at Trattoria del Ponte Lungo. The tortellini in brodo are delicious, but you might also be tempted by the tagliatelle con ragu. You take the same bus (13, 81, 87, 91) as you would take to get to the supermarket, and get off at the Ponte Lungo stop. They are open for lunch and dinner Monday through Friday, but their schedule can vary on weekends and holidays, so call ahead. And don't forget that the dinner hour starts much later in Italy, say 7:00, so you won't find them open before that. The atmosphere is casual, with family groups and after-work dinner parties equally welcome, and the rates are very reasonable. And if you find you're at a loss as to how to proceed with all the wonderful choices on the menu, the wait staff are more than happy to help.

12. Have a Cocktail Before Dinner the Bolognese Way

Perhaps the most Bolognese of traditions is the aperitivo, which generally starts around 6:00, and kicks off the evening, or winds up a busy day. The best place in Bologna to go for this sociable and light-hearted daily event is Café Pasticceria Gamberini on Via Ugo Bassi, right in the center of town. Don't be put off by the cost of your cocktail; it will seem steep at first, no matter what you order. Just keep in mind that the price includes a plateful of gourmet appetizers, and in my experience, those "snacks" are often so good and so filling, you may skip dinner and move right on to dessert!

13. Get Around by Bus

The buses in Bologna will get you anywhere you need to go. You can purchase a ticket at any tabaccheria (which will have a sign above the door with a large capital T on a blue background.) You have a few options depending on your needs, from one-fare tickets, to monthly passes, and keep in mind that many buses travel well outside the center into the countryside and therefore may cost more than the regular fare. Some buses have ticket machines on board, but the fare will be more expensive, they're not on every bus, and they don't always work. Remember to validate your ticket every time you get on the bus, even if it's a monthly pass that you already "activated", and even if you change busses in the course of your journey; you'll see the machine just beyond the driver's seat when you get on. Either way, make sure you've paid the fare. Fines for being without a ticket when plain-clothes inspectors board the bus are very steep. Italian bus strikes are infamous, and Bologna is not immune, but they are generally announced in advance. And a word on Italian bus etiquette: you get on the bus at the front or the back, and you get off via the doors in the middle.

14. Get to the Airport

Guglielmo Marconi Airport is relatively small and easy to get to and to navigate. While it's important to leave enough time for your flights and transfers, you can rest easy in the knowledge that you won't be spending time taking a train from one terminal to another or walking for 20 minutes. Marconi's just not that big. You can take the Aerobus, which makes limited stops between the airport and the train station, or you can take a taxi, but I've found that ordering a car ahead – known locally as a "macchina blu" or blue car - is far more economical, convenient, and reliable.

15. *Walk Around, Literally*

Perhaps the best way to be part of Bologna is to walk it. The city is not really that large, and it's almost impossible to get lost. Originally surrounded by a wall to keep "bad guys" out, and the "good guys" safe, Bologna is circular and planned like a bicycle wheel, so that each of the main streets spreads out from the center. Some of the original "porte" (gates) remain, each with its unique personality, and you may enjoy a walk along what remains of the city wall and these gates. I'd invite you too, if you're going to be in town for any length of time, to watch any of the gates and see if you can divine a schedule for when and why the wooden doors inside the gates are opened or closed. In the over 14 years I lived there, I was never able to figure it out and neither were any of my local friends. Maybe you will solve this mystery for me!

16. Get Your Day Started the Way the Locals Do

And that means a trip to the bar (as coffee shops are known in Italy) for caffé, "spremuto" of fresh squeezed orange juice, and a brioche. Try Antico Caffe' Scaletto on Via Ugo Bassi. It's right in the center and is frequented by the locals who know. But no matter where you go, there are generally two systems for this morning ritual. Either you walk right up to the bar, order, and enjoy your breakfast as you are jostled by hungry locals ready for their own cappuccinos, and then pay as you leave. Or, you pay at the register first, take your receipt to the bar, give it to the barista who will then put a rip in it, and proceed as before. You'll be able to tell If latter method is how it works in any given bar, because the floor will be littered with the tattered receipts.

17. Shop Downtown

As with any city, there are plenty of shops. Via dell'Indipendenza is the main drag, and you will find a plethora of options, from clothing to perfumeries to hand bags and shoes in all price ranges. It's important to keep in mind, however, that unlike in America, having a receipt and a change of heart over a purchase, does not mean you will get a refund. In some cases, you will be able to make an exchange or get a store credit, but not always. Be sure you're happy with what you're buying, because you will not be able to get your money back.

18. Watch Bologna's Wealthiest Residents Do Their Shopping

If you'd like to have a peek at how the other half lives in Bologna, there's the shopping "sotto i portici" in Piazza Maggiore. If you are standing facing San Petronio, you'll have the pedestrian Via d'Azeglio to your right, and Via Archiginnasio to your left with a defined sidewalk and Bologna's classic porticoest. A walk along either will reveal eye-popping prices and boutique-style shopping of a bygone era. The window-dressing is often unbelievably imaginative and whimsical, and the people-watching is just as much fun as any shopping you might or might not be able to do there.

19. Find Anything and Everything for Sale

Every Friday and Saturday, rain or shine, the market, known as "Piazzola" in Bologna, takes over the parking lot on the corner of Via Indipendenza and Via Irnerio. And you can find absolutely anything there: clothes -from intimates to winter jackets- leather goods, toiletries, all manner of housewares, jewelry, sewing supplies, and more. The stalls are generally grouped by product, and they are in the same place week to week. You can get excellent deals for quality merchandise and at the same time find "five and dime" items on the cheap, in case you need a pair of shoelaces or a pair of socks.

20. Be Serenaded on the Cheap

Speaking of walking the streets of Bologna, a stroll down Via Zamboni, which starts at the foot of the two towers, will take you into the heart of the university district and Piazza Verdi. If you like opera, or any kind of classical music, try to stop by. There are a number of bars and pubs where you can take a seat and soak up the intellectual buzz, but the best part is in the warmer months when the Teatro Communale di Bologna has the windows open and you can hear vocalists rehearsing. It's an amazing experience, made even more impressive by the fact that the locals seem absolutely unimpressed as they get on with their day.

"Bologna is the best city in Italy for food and has the least number of tourists. With its medieval beauty, it has it all." – Mario Batali

21. Look After Yourself

There's no doubt that the life of a traveler is exciting, but sometimes the common cold, or an upset stomach will interfere. There's no reason to let that ruin an otherwise great trip! Most pharmacies in Bologna take turns as to which are open on nights, weekends, or lunchtimes (which can run as long as three hours.) The Farmacia Comunale in Piazza Maggiore is the exception. You can count on it to be open, 24 hours a day, seven days a week, 365 days a year. So rest easy in the knowledge that two aspirin and the advice of helpful pharmacists is always available.

22. Watch a Movie Outside in Piazza Maggiore

Once the weather turns warmer, Bologna sets up an outdoor cinema, right in its main square, complete with a giant movie screen, stage, and chairs. There is usually a theme of some kind, and occasionally the stars or people involved in the making of some of the films will be on hand for its showing, especially if the film has some special connection to Bologna. The movies begin around 9:45, and there will be something for everyone, including some original language films.

23. Get Yourself Some Watermelon

Bologna gets very hot and very humid in the Summertime, but fortunately, temporary watermelon bars pop up around the city. Once the sun goes down, you will find many a local enjoying a slice of ice-cold watermelon both in town and on the outskirts, where a refreshing breeze will be blowing that seemed unimaginable only an hour or two before. No need to dress up. Let the juice drip down your arm! Everyone understands.

24. Find Venice without Leaving Bologna

Bologna was once a fresh water port, but over the centuries, the city built up over the waterways. Without an underground tour of the city, or a trip to the outskirts where you can see locals sunning themselves along the river and tributaries, you'd never suspect that there are canals running right under the city. But you can find them if you know where to look. Head down Via Indipendenza from Piazza Nettuno, and turn right onto Via Righi. Now keep your eyes open. You will see glimpses of the canals to your right. Turn right again onto Via Piella, and you will see what appears to be an alley to your left, but if you look down, you'll see the canal running happily along. On the other side of the street is a window in the wall, the "finestrella di Via Piella," and here again, you will see this little Venice, right in the heart of Bologna.

25. Get Political

You may have heard a bit about Italian politics. It can be kind of intense, but all the rancor is put aside for the Festa dell'Unita'. Organized annually by the Pd or Partita Democratica, absolustely everybody goes to a unity festival, at some point over the Spring and Summer, at least for the traditional games and food, if not for the party speeches. They run the gamut from a countryside celebration that takes up a weekend or two, to the Festa dell'Unita that takes over the Parco Nord fair grounds and lasts for over three weeks from August to September. There is a carnival-like atmosphere to all of them, with vendors, and games of chance, and rides, and of course food. Go to any one of these and enjoy the classic tortellini "con panna" - with cream - most likely made by someone's grandmother that very day. No one will care about your political affiliations.

26. Climb the Towers of Bologna

Bologna used to have towers everywhere, often connected by walkways, all of which served as a form of lookout, and a sign of the wealth and power of the family who owned and lived in them. Today, there are only a few left behind, some of which you can stay in if you choose, but the two central towers are the most famous symbols of Bologna itself, and the taller of the two, Degli Asinelli can be climbed via an internal staircase. Everyone does it, locals and tourists alike, and the view from the top is breathtaking. But be careful if you happen to be studying at the University of Bologna. Legend has it that you'll never graduate if you climb the tower before you've received your degree.

27. Walk the Giardini Margherita

Just south of the center of the city lies its most famous park. Stretching from Porta Castiglione to Porta Santo Stefano (and across the viale, the road that rings the city) are the Giardini Margherita. It's an expansive park that includes a pond with turtles and fish, gelato stands, a coffee shop, and a number of children's rides. Enjoy a picnic lunch on the grounds, or a walk, and listen to the sounds of the Bolognesi enjoying a day out. Go at the end of May and early June, and you will be enveloped in the smell of flowering trees and plants.

28. Take a Hike in the City

If you feel the need to get some aerobic exercise, why not strap on your sneakers and head for San Luca. Another of the traditional symbols of Bologna, the 18th century basilica sits atop the Colle della Guardia, 300 meters above the city. From Porta Saragozza, walk along Via Saragozza until you reach Arco del Meloncello. From there you just keep your feet moving as you follow the 666 porticos that lead you to the top. Easier said than done, perhaps, but it's definitely doable, and you'll have the added motivation of seeing the view once you reach to top. And of course, you'll have made room for lunch when you come back down.

29. See Bologna Underground

Part of Bologna's mystique lies beneath it. From the Roman bridges, to the steps used by washer women in days gone by, an underground tour of the city is fascinating, if a little unnerving and sometimes smelly. There are seasonal restrictions, since you will be walking along an underground river, and the tours are occasionally suspended for this reason and/or for renovations. Get in touch with the Bologna Welcome tourist office to be sure of their schedule.

30. Cook Tortellini Yourself

Are you craving tortellini in the city that invented them? Of course you are! And you're in just the right place to find them. In Bologna, even the supermarket versions are excellent, but I suspect you are looking for those individually packaged little baggies that look like they came out of your grandmother's kitchen. So, you can head down Via Clavature from Piazza Maggiore, and stop in at any shop where you see pasta. Or you can go directly to Tamburini on Via Caprarie (only a turn or two further on) and go straight to heaven. And if you are thinking of taking a bit of the tastes of Italy with you when you leave, the folks at Tamburini will also be able to help you with appropriate packaging for the flight home.

"In the new era, thought itself will be transmitted by radio." – Guglielmo Marconi

EMILY MATHEWS

31. Take a Whack at Crescentine, and Enjoy

Get ready for a culinary treat. Crescentine are basically small fried dough squares. You order them according to how many people are in your party. A few moments later, the crescentine as well as cold cuts, cheeses and pickled vegetables will appear at your table and the fun begins. You take your crescentina and whack it with your fork to get the air out of it, then you spread on the cheese, or fold in the prosciutto, maybe add a pickled onion and take a bite. When you've had your fill of the savory, the waitress will return and ask if you'd like more of the crescentine or if you'd like to finish off whatever remains with Nutella or jam, and the whole process begins again. You can find restaurants that serve them all over Bologna, but Le Due Porte on Via Del Pratello, is your best bet. The street is mostly pedestrian and is home to one eatery after another, most with outdoor seating in the warmer months.

32. Find a Special Gift

Located inside the foot of the tower Degli Asinelli, on Strada Maggiore, ArtigianArte is shop of handmade art. There are ornaments, figurines, jewelry, plaques, and more. I wandered in when a particular piece caught my eye, never expecting to find anything more than overpriced items catering to tourists. What I found was a very reasonably priced, handmade gift for my mother's birthday. While the shopkeepers are surely used to tourists, they are also clearly enthusiastic about the artists who show their wares in this unique tower shop and happy to help out the curious shopper, no matter where you're from.

33. Browse an Old Fashioned Hardware Store

Just past the two towers on Strada Maggiore, lies the Ferramenta Castaldini. The shop window is bursting with kitchen gadgets, and utensils, and cookie cutters, and more. Step inside and you will find the store itself just as full, and patrons lined up to ask the informed and ever-patient staff for whatever it is they need. Many of the items are still kept in cardboard "drawers" that make up the wall behind the counter, and even if you don't find yourself in need of a washer or a set of pliers, there is plenty to see in this old fashioned but clearly vital hardware store.

34. Spend the Holidays in Bologna

You are in for a special treat. The streets are festooned with lights, a different design for each of the main thoroughfares, and the lights that hang from Bologna's classic porticos are often decorated too. There is a tree in Piazza Nettuno, and the Santa Lucia Christmas Market on Strada Maggiore. This market is over two hundred years old and runs from mid-November to just before the Epiphany. You will find all kinds of holiday decorations and gifts, as well as read- to-eat treats like candied nuts and marzipan fruits, and of course, figurines and accessories for the family nativity. The Italians love their manger scenes, often building them in such dimensions as to take over entire corners of their homes, and in Bologna, of course, no nativity is complete without a tortellini maker and a butcher selling mortadella.

35. Meet at Nettuno

Bologna really isn't that big a city, and you'll probably start seeing some familiar faces after only a short time. So if you've made some friends, or your party has decided to split up for the afternoon, you can count on EVERYONE meeting at Piazza Nettuno. At the juncture of Via Indipendenza, Via Ugo Bassi, and Via Rizzoli, this square is home to the fountain statue of Neptune and is really the most convenient place to meet. Centrally located, just off Piazza Maggiore, Piazza Nettuno puts you in the middle of everything, including multiple bus lines, should you need to get somewhere else, once your group has gathered. Hang around and watch how many folks are meeting up "at Nettuno" while you wait for your friends and feel the heartbeat of Bologna.

36. *Visit Piazza Maggiore*

This is the very heart of Bologna. Piazza Maggiore is home to San Petronio, a church at one time designed in the hopes of outshining St. Peter's in Rome, where you can still attend mass. To your left are the tiny streets that will take you to the tortellini shops and a place to sit for a glass of prosecco as you watch the passing parade. To your right, you'll see the Comunale and the Salaborsa, with Palazzo Re Enzo at your back. And there in the middle of it all is the great curbed square, where children play, and students study, families meet, and rallies are held. Don't walk across it on the diagonal though. Much like climbing the Degli Asinelli tower, this too is considered bad luck if you have yet to graduate from university.

37. Enjoy Long Weekends in the Springtime

The Monday after Easter, or Pasquetta, is always a day off. The kids are off from school, and virtually everything is closed. This is true all over Italy (and many other places too, I'm sure.) But if you are lucky, you will find that Pasquetta falls closely to two other holidays which are near and dear to the Bolognese heart: Liberation Day on April 25, and Labor Day on May 1., known to one and all simply by their dates. April 25 commemorates the end of World War II and is particularly poignant to the Bolognesi not only because many of the older generation remember watching the liberating armies march through the city gates, but because the Resistance was very strong in this northern town, and the people suffered greatly because of it. May 1, is a holiday honoring the worker, and given Bologna's history and politics over the years, Labor Day here will involve multiple rallies and marches for workers' rights. People plan long weekends, or walks through town, and on these two holidays, you will get a real glimpse of Italians and the Bolognesi in particular celebrating who they are.

38. Be in the Know in Children's Books

The Fiera in Bologna is an enormous complex of trade-show pavilions which host numerous fairs throughout the year. One of the most important, and world famous to boot, is the Bologna Children's Book Fair. Held in the Springtime, this fair attracts everyone in the children's literature industry, from authors and illustrators to publishers and book vendors. I had the great good fortune to attend once as an interpreter for a budding author/graphic artist, and was overwhelmed by the fantasy and imagination that runs wild at this annual event. And if you attend towards the end, you might come away with some first run, prototypes of books that will one day hit the shelves.

39. Get a Burger – Italian Style?

You may be in the food capital of Italy, but that doesn't mean you won't get a hankering for the tastes of home. If you find you need a burger-fix, keep the Roadhouse Restaurant in mind. The first steakhouse chain in Italy, it offers American style menu items (and décor) with Italian flare. I am by no means a committed carnivore, but I've never had a better burger than those I've eaten at the Roadhouse. It's not a cheap meal, so keep that in mind, but the quality of the food is excellent, and you definitely get what you pay for. The Bologna Roadhouse is located next to the Fiera, and while you might expect this to mean the place is constantly packed with tourists, the grand majority of the patrons are Italians, including family groups.

40. Start Your Engines at the Ducati Museum

Bologna is home to one of the world's most famous motorcycles: Ducati. And the Bolognesi love it. The plant is located in the section of Bologna known as Borgo Panigale. When a Ducati is competing in one of the MOTO GP or WSBK races, the announcers will often refer to it as the motorcycle "from the Borgo", and I believe all of Bologna swells with pride to hear it. You can tour both the factory (with a guide) and the museum. Getting there is easy on public transportation, as Ducati is located just off the Via Emilia, and a number of buses will take you there. If you're a fan of racing, this may be a pilgrimage for you, but even if you're not, the history of the company and what it's meant to the region is something to see. The company has, on occasion, set up TV screens for folks to watch important races right from the factory. Even if you're not into motorcycles, the experience is great, and besides, the races don't last all that long.

"The perfect life is the combination of great moments and bad ones, and under that point of view, my life is fantastic, because I've certainly hit more than one bump." – Alex Zanardi

41. Listen to a Quiet City

Back in the day, virtually all businesses in Italy would shut down for the entire month of August. That is no longer the case, but two weeks of vacation somewhere around Ferragosto (technically the Feast of the Assumption) on August 15 is still the standard for most Italians. Bologna is no exception. Everybody gets out of town, more than a few shops will shutter their storefronts, and you will have the city to yourself. This also means that the buses run on a reduced schedule, and some services –including emergency care- will be more limited; but barring a complete disaster, you will see Bologna at her most welcoming. Get yourself some groceries to limit surprises if it turns out your favorite eatery is closed for a few days, pack yourself a sandwich, and walk around. Without the hustle and bustle of typical city life, there is more to hear. The only time you'll find the city LESS crowded, is if Italy is playing in the World Cup!

42. Dress for All Seasons

While the Bolognesi have a knack for fashion, what may be of more concern to you as you visit Bologna, is the weather. Bologna never gets truly cold. Temperatures don't fall below freezing too often, and when they do, it's not by much. It is, however, a very damp city, with lots of medieval buildings made of stone. You may find that you don't really need your heavy winter coat to walk around outside, but an extra cardigan will be useful once you get indoors. They have a real Spring, complete with April showers and May flowers, usually right on schedule. But in the Summers, even the fish sweat; what was cold and damp in the Winter, becomes hazy, hot, and oppressively humid in the Summer, with temperatures well over 100F all day into early evening. The Autumn tends to be balmy well into October, with dense fog a common occurrence and a driving hazard by November. But by then, there are chestnuts roasting on every corner, and novello wines being served, and the mist just adds to the mystery of this medieval city.

43. Learn Some Bulgnais

The Bolognesi are very proud of their city and its identity as an intellectual and cultural center. Part of what sets them apart from other Italians is their dialect: Bulgnais. There are many opinions in all regions of Italy as to whether and how much of the dialects should be preserved. In Bologna, the local dialect is not taught in the schools, but you can take classes and purchase Italian – Buglnais dictionaries. You certainly don't need to know the local dialect in order to get by while visiting Bologna, but I highly recommend taking in some theater in dialect at Teatro Alemanni on Vla Mazzini. It's outside the city walls, easily accesslble by public transportation, and while you might not understand a word of what's going on, the experience of sitting among the Bolognesi who do understand it will give you a real sense of who they are. And if it should come up that you are there to hear their beloved dialect, I suspect you will be welcomed with open arms and find yourself in the midst ot at least 5 "experts" who want to explain it all to you. Enjoy!

44. Go to the Library

The Biblioteca Salaborsa is the city library of Bologna. Making up one side of Piazza Nettuno, it's easy to get to, and you will be able to find all kinds of reading materials in a number of languages there. In recent years there a few shops have gone in as well, and while they tend to be a bit pricey, browsing in this palazzo is an experience of itself. The most particular part, however, is the floor. When you enter, you have to choose to go around to the right or the left. Either is fine, and then continue straight ahead to the main room with the aforementioned shops. Now look down. The flooring is largely see-through, and you can see the ruins that the current structure was built upon. It's a bit unnerving at first, but once you get used to it, it's fascinating!

45. Explore Other Cities

Bologna is centrally located and has a busy train station, Bologna Centrale. You can get anywhere from there. With the high-speed trains, Rome is only two hours away; Milan and Rimini (on the Adriatic) are about an hour's ride; Venice will take about 90 minutes; and Florence can be reached in just 30 minutes. You can easily take day trips to some of Italy's other cities and towns from your home base in Bologna, one of the peninsula's less frequented treasures. The station itself is beautiful, as old fashioned European train stations tend to be, and while your Italian may not be good enough to understand the announcements over the loudspeakers (that particular trick took me years!) the signage is excellent, so pack your day bag and a snack and explore!

46. *Prepare for the Befana*

Just when you thought the holidays were over with the last of the New Year's Revelers trudging home to bed, you discover that there is one last bit of holiday cheer on its way. And that cheer is none other than the Befana. She is an old crone, who rides a broom into children's rooms – via the window - on January 6 and leaves sweet treats for the good little boys and girls and a lump of coal for the naughty. If you are in Bologna over the holidays, you will see Befana decorating shop windows, and in every sweet shop and Christmas market, but it's not till after January 1 that she really steals the show. Some of the renditions are meticulously detailed and would be just as well suited for Halloween decorations. The kids are out of school till at least January 6, depending on where it falls in the work week, and the adults have the day off for the Epiphany and one last holiday meal. Parents fill stockings, and kids leave a snack for this wise old woman.

47. Try These Paper-Thin, Fried Pastries

Once the Befana has come and gone on January 6, the holidays are well and truly over. Schools reopen, folks go back to work, and it's a long hard slog, with nary a long weekend in sight till Easter Monday. You may be thinking that this is not a good time to visit Bologna. On the contrary, now is when you get to enjoy sfrappole! These light and crispy fried dough sweets are only around for Carnival, which technically runs from January 7 till Fat Tuesday. Easy to make if you have access to a kitchen –or a cook willing to teach you- and even easier to find in bakeries all over Bologna, they start appearing in the supermarkets and cafés by mid to late January, usually around the time everyone has finished their holiday leftovers and people are ready for a little mid-Winter pick-me-up.

48. Go to a Carnival Party

While Bologna itself is not famous for its Carnival festivities, it does have a parade on or near Fat Tuesday, culminating at Piazza Maggiore, and the kids enjoy it. You can easily get to Venice from Bologna by train, and that has its own, more dramatic and adult mystique. I don't recommend making the trip during the week leading up to Mardi Gras, as the crowds are overwhelming enough to take away from the wonder of it all. If you are interested in celebrating Carnival, get yourself to Cento in the Ferrara area. The Cento Carnevale d'Europa has something for everyone. It may take a bit of doing to get there, but the trip is well worth it..

49. Rest Easy and Eat Breakfast

If you're looking for more traditional lodging in Bologna (and you don't need the Italian lessons offered in tip number 1), you'll have your pick in any price range, from luxury hotels on Via dell'Indipendenza, to Airbnb options all over the city. One drawback is that during trade shows, which Bologna hosts often, a room can be very hard to find. You may want to keep this in mind when planning your trip. That said, once you've found accommodations, if your breakfast is included in your hotel fee, you can count on starting your day well fed. The "continental" breakfast goes beyond yogurt, coffee, and a muffin. There is usually quite a spread, including cold cuts, and heartier breads, and sometimes some American-style breakfast items like eggs and bacon.

50. See Marzabotto

You cannot escape history in Bologna, or anywhere in Italy for that matter, but if you'd like to see a bit of the surrounding countryside of Bologna, a trip to Marzabotto, may be the trip for you. Easily reached by train or bus, and about 17 miles from the Center of Bologna, Marzabotto is vitally important to the Bolognesi for two reasons. The first is the part it played in World War II, the second is a complete Etruscan town! Enjoy the ride out to Marzabotto and a few hours walking around what remains of this ancient village. There is also a museum with excavated items which is open year round.

> TOURIST

Greater than a Tourist

Please read other Greater than a Tourist Books.

Join the >Tourist Mailing List :
http://eepurl.com/cxspyf

Facebook:
https://www.facebook.com/GreaterThanATourist

Pinterest:
http://pinterest.com/GreaterThanATourist

Instagram:
http://Instagram.com/GreaterThanATourist

Please leave your honest review of this book on Amazon and Goodreads. Thank you.

Made in the USA
Middletown, DE
16 August 2017